The Memling Museum–St John's Hospital
Bruges

Irene Smets

The Memling Museum–St John's Hospital Bruges

Ludion

FOREWORD

People have come knocking on the doors of St John's Hospital for many centuries now, not only in search of shelter but also to admire the art treasures that it houses. The historic buildings, which are among the oldest in Europe, the grounds and the impressive archive form a truly exceptional ensemble.

In 1839, as visitor pressure intensified, the then 'Commission for Civil Almshouses' decided to open 'St John's Hospital Museum'. The institution proved an immediate success. Both the historical setting and the treasures within captured the public imagination. The six works by Hans Memling – four of which were actually commissioned by hospital brothers and sisters – made a key contribution to the rediscovery of the 'Flemish Primitives'. The image of Bruges cultivated by the Romantics was inseparably linked to St John's Hospital and Memling's paintings. The museum has, of course, developed a great deal since it opened in 1839, since when public interest has continued to grow.

Bruges City Council took the decision several years ago to begin the large-scale restoration of the historic buildings, with the dual intention of preserving this unique piece of Flemish architectural heritage and ensuring that the museum could meet the necessary modern technical standards.

We are grateful to Ludion for publishing this guide to coincide with the reopening of the museum. Its layout follows the new, themed approach, key works of art are examined in greater detail and ample attention is paid to the beautifully restored rooms, some of which have been incorporated in the visitor circuit for the first time. It was a particular pleasure to work with Irene Smets, author of this attractively presented guide. With her fluent and enjoyable style, she introduces one of Europe's most individual museums to the visitors who come to Bruges from all over the world.

p. 1 Hans Memling, *Triptych of St John the Baptist and St John the Evangelist*, detail (see p. 37).

p. 2 View from the bridge over the Reie in Mariastraat: the south façade of the hospital (14th century) and the convent (16th century). The smaller structures at the front date from the 19th century.

Hans Memling, *Triptych of St John the Baptist and St John the Evangelist*, detail (see p. 37).

Hilde Lobelle-Caluwé
Curator

5

St John's Hospital, with its wards, church, monastery and convent, is one of the most attractive medieval buildings of its type anywhere in Europe. For 700 years – from 1150 to 1864 – it served as a charitable institution, caring for the sick and the needy. The site originally included sheds, stables, a brewery, a bakery, a cemetery and chapel, an orchard, a kitchen garden and a vegetable garden – all for the use of the hospital and its religious community. These were all removed around 1850, however, to make way for the new hospital complex that remained in operation from 1864 to 1976, and which now houses the information, art and conference centre known as 'Oud Sint-Jan'. Although the main buildings are all that has survived of the medieval hospital, they still form an extremely impressive ensemble.

The architectural history of the complex can be read from its façade on Mariastraat. The Romanesque pointed gable incorporating the entrance gate dates from the 13th century. The carved tympanum above the porch was added a little later – towards the end of the 13th century – although it was restored in 1911–13, when a bluestone vestibule was added. The pointed gable on the left, with its four large windows, was built in the Gothic style in the 13th century. The tower and the monastery, to the right of the hospital building, also date from the 13th century, but the solid architecture of its façade is still entirely Romanesque. The three-sided apse of the hospital church, located between the central ward and the monastery, was built in the 15th century.

It is worth taking a moment to walk through the monastery gate, alongside the Romanesque tower, and to go through to the rear. Here you can admire the hospital's 13th- and 14th-century west façades, with the chapel and monastery on the left and the convent buildings on the right, which are still home to a group of nuns. Further in the distance, looking towards Zonneke Meers, you will see all that remains of the branch of the Reie that once curved through the hospital grounds. A small stretch of the river still runs beneath the wards.

A picturesque view of the side of the hospital and the convent buildings can also be had from the bridge in Mariastraat.

Anonymous, *The Cemetery Chapel at St John's Hospital*, 18th century, panel, 65 x 40.2 cm. This little painting calls on the passer-by to show charity. Donations were used to finance memorial masses for the very poorest citizens, who were buried in straw. *(Wards)*

The 13th- and 14th-century west façades. This attractive architectural ensemble illustrates the evolution from Romanesque to early Gothic architecture in Bruges.

Façade on Mariastraat, 13th–14th century, with later modifications.

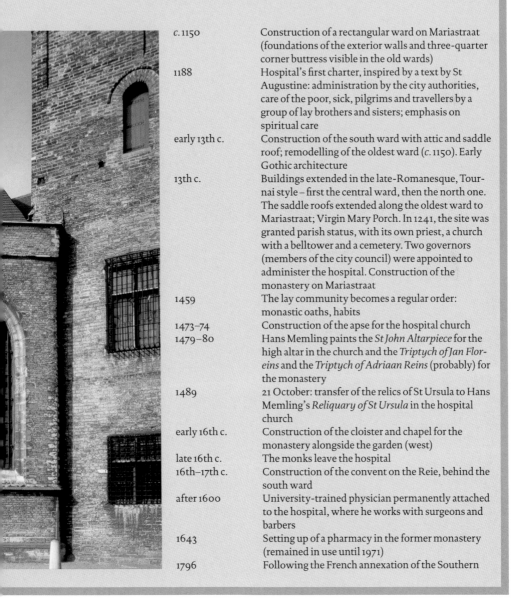

c. 1150	Construction of a rectangular ward on Mariastraat (foundations of the exterior walls and three-quarter corner buttress visible in the old wards)
1188	Hospital's first charter, inspired by a text by St Augustine: administration by the city authorities, care of the poor, sick, pilgrims and travellers by a group of lay brothers and sisters; emphasis on spiritual care
early 13th c.	Construction of the south ward with attic and saddle roof; remodelling of the oldest ward (*c.* 1150). Early Gothic architecture
13th c.	Buildings extended in the late-Romanesque, Tournai style – first the central ward, then the north one. The saddle roofs extended along the oldest ward to Mariastraat; Virgin Mary Porch. In 1241, the site was granted parish status, with its own priest, a church with a belltower and a cemetery. Two governors (members of the city council) were appointed to administer the hospital. Construction of the monastery on Mariastraat
1459	The lay community becomes a regular order: monastic oaths, habits
1473–74	Construction of the apse for the hospital church
1479–80	Hans Memling paints the *St John Altarpiece* for the high altar in the church and the *Triptych of Jan Floreins* and the *Triptych of Adriaan Reins* (probably) for the monastery
1489	21 October: transfer of the relics of St Ursula to Hans Memling's *Reliquary of St Ursula* in the hospital church
early 16th c.	Construction of the cloister and chapel for the monastery alongside the garden (west)
late 16th c.	The monks leave the hospital
16th–17th c.	Construction of the convent on the Reie, behind the south ward
after 1600	University-trained physician permanently attached to the hospital, where he works with surgeons and barbers
1643	Setting up of a pharmacy in the former monastery (remained in use until 1971)
1796	Following the French annexation of the Southern

	Netherlands, the administration of Bruges' charitable institutions is taken over by the 'Commission for Civil Almshouses'
1806–35	The Ecole Départementale de Médecine takes up residence at St John's Hospital. Its doctors and surgeons act as lecturers and the medieval cemetery chapel is turned into an anatomy theatre
1815	Memling's *Diptych of Maarten van Nieuwenhove* (1487) and *Portrait of a Young Woman* (1480) are presented to St John's Hospital
1839	Creation of a *Cabinet de Tableaux* in the former Superior's Room in the convent: permanently open to the public, with part of the hospital's art collection, it was one of Bruges' first museums
1864	New hospital comes into operation on the site. Medieval wards cleared out. Church remains in use
1891	Restoration of the old buildings (architect Louis Delacenserie). The restored *Cabinet de Tableaux* is now used exclusively to display Memling's paintings, a few pieces of furniture and precious objects. The portraits of the governors of St John's Hospital and St Julian's Hospital are hung in the pharmacy's drawing room
1925	The administration of Bruges' charitable institutions passes to the Commission for Public Assistance (in 1976 this became the OCMW – Public Centre for Social Welfare)
1939	Memling exhibition at the Municipal Museums of Bruges. The room in the convent containing the Memling paintings is henceforward known as the 'Memling Museum'
1950 and beyond	Conversion of the wards, gradual transformation into museum
1972	The 17th-century pharmacy, the Governors' Chamber (the pharmacy's drawing room) and the monastery building are added to the museum
1976	The 19th-century hospital is closed down (replaced by the Algemeen Ziekenhuis Sint-Jan in the Sint-Pieters district of the city)
1990	Administration of the Memling Museum–St John's Hospital transferred from the OCMW to the Municipal Museums of Bruges
1983–2000	A series of restoration projects returns the medieval St John's Hospital closer to its original state

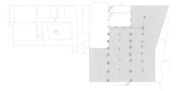

Remains of the foundations and a corner buttress from the original ward (c. 1150) and fragment of the original floor of the south ward (14th century). In the middle there is a pillar measuring over 20 metres in height that was cut from a single, gigantic tree.

The moment you enter St John's Hospital through the Virgin Mary Porch, you are struck by the panoramic space that unfolds before you. It is certainly an impressive way to welcome visitors. From your raised vantage point on the steps, you are offered an overall impression of the medieval hospital and its special atmosphere.

The museum located in the former wards provides a glimpse of hospital life from the Middle Ages to the late 18th century – a life that remained largely unchanged in all that time. It was only in the 19th century that medicine began to progress rapidly and new discover-

ies were widely applied in medical practice.

A number of themes are explored through the many valuable works of art, pieces of furniture and utensils that have found their way into the hospital over the years. They include the charitable institution in medieval Bruges, the grounds and historical buildings of St John's Hospital, the layout of the wards, administration, staff, care of the sick and care of the soul, and death.

St John's Hospital underwent countless architectural modifications during its existence. This is already plain from the exterior, but can be seen even more clearly as you tour the inside of the buildings. There are traces everywhere of modifications and extensions – bricked-up windows and doors, alterations to the archways, ceilings and fireplaces that have been removed, and a 13th-century exterior wall (with drips around the windows etc.) that was soon transformed into an interior wall. There is a lot to discover if you take your time and look carefully.

Charitable institutions in medieval Bruges

Hospitals arose in Western Europe during the early Middle Ages. They were not hospitals in the sense that we know today, but 'guesthouses' providing hospitality to pilgrims, travellers, the poor and the sick. Institutions of this kind were often linked to monasteries – monks were, after all, obliged by the Rule of St Benedict to offer charity and hospitality: 'Let all guests who arrive be received like Christ, for He shall say, "I came as a guest, and you received Me."'

As towns developed in the 12th century, the civic authorities or prominent citizens founded new charitable institutions, as there was a need within the urban community for a social safety-net for the destitute and for strangers. In the course of the 12th century, Bruges evolved into one of the most important cities in the world – a fact reflected in the foundation there of several charitable institutions. St John's Hospital was the first, followed in the 13th century by the Potterie and later by homes for the elderly, prostitutes, foundlings, the mentally ill and lepers – for everyone, in short, who found themselves in need. All of these houses were administered by the civic authorities.

Friendship Cup, Southern Netherlands, 1664, engraved glass, faience, silver gilt and copper. Six medallions are engraved in the goblet: the Bruges municipal arms, the crowned 'B' for Bruges and the emblems of St John's Hospital, Magdalene Hospice (for lepers), St Julian's Hospital and the Potterie. The text *eendraecht mackt maecht* ('unity is strength') is inscribed around the rim. According to tradition, the cup was used to drink a toast whenever a new head was appointed to one of the municipal hospitals.

Anonymous, *The West Façade of St John's Hospital*, 18th century, canvas, 168 x 245 cm. The painting offers a lively picture of the hospital site and its rural character. The branch of the Reie that flows in a wide curve around the hospital grounds includes a ford and a washing place. A small structure has been built against the north wall for drying the washing. Hospital residents walk around the grounds dressed in red and blue jackets – Bruges' municipal colours.

Site, buildings and name

St John's Hospital is one of the largest sites within the City of Bruges. It was named 'Domus Beati Johannis' (the house of St John), after John the Evangelist, to whom it was dedicated. The other biblical St John – the Baptist – was adopted as a second patron later in the Middle Ages, since when the two saints' respective emblems – a lamb and a poisoned chalice – formed the hospital's symbol, appearing on countless utensils and pieces of furniture.

Nowadays, the hospital is located in the heart of the city, but in the Middle Ages it stood at the periphery, just within the city boundary traced by the Reie. The main entrance of the hospital and the monastery opened onto Maria-straat – an important thoroughfare leading to the town centre. The courtyard to the rear, the cemetery,

the orchard, the gardens and the outbuildings stretched off into the low-lying grassland. Over the centuries, however, the land around the hospital was gradually swallowed up as the city expanded.

St John Plate, Flanders, early 16th century, painted wood. Plates like this showing the severed head of John the Baptist began to be produced in the Middle Ages for devotional purposes. The saint was invoked for a variety of reasons, including the cure of head and throat complaints. The image comes from the story of St John's execution in the Bible.

Emblem of St John's Hospital, stamped and gilded motif on the leather back of a Baroque chair, second half 17th century.

Administration

The hospital was administered by the civic authorities from the very beginning. The city council drew up its rules and regulations and appointed its staff. From the 13th century onwards, two prominent citizens were selected as governors to oversee the day-to-day activities of the hospital, which were performed by the monks and nuns attached to it. This arrangement persisted until the region's occupation by revolutionary France, when general administration was placed in the hands of the Commission for Civil Almshouses. Social Services took responsibility for the hospital in the 20th century, until 1990, when the institution became part of the Municipal Museums of Bruges.

The male religious community at the hospital was headed by a 'Master', who was responsible for managing its income and expenditure, and for the maintenance of its property. The sisters, meanwhile, were under the authority of a 'Mistress'. It was their job to care for the sick and to perform domestic duties, assisted by a number of maids and servants. The brothers occupied themselves with the administrative and financial side of the hospital's activities. When the male community was dissolved towards the end of the 16th century, the Mistress and a lay receiver took over the Master's former duties.

Rules of St John's Hospital, 1188, parchment. This is the earliest surviving copy of the hospital's rules. The Latin text specifies how hospital staff were to live, dealing with such things as prayers, dress, behaviour at table, fasting, punishment of misdemeanours and conditions for admission to the community.

Income

National government in the Middle Ages was nowhere near as centralised and organised as it is today – there were no central subsidies or other financial assistance, for instance, and cities and important institutions fiercely defended their independence. As a result, hospitals and other charitable bodies had to fend for themselves. St John's Hospital derived its income from charges, gifts, bequests, taxes and duties, and the money it earned from its fishponds, woods (woodcutting), peat pits (peat or turf was used as a fuel) and farms.

Surveyors at work, detail from Anthonis Messiaens and Heindryck de la Porte's *Map of the Land Belonging to Ter Lepe Farm*, 1658, parchment. The Ter Lepe estate in Aartrijke-Zedelgem, with its fields, woods and meadows, belonged to the hospital.

Two clerics, the Mistress and a hospital governor, detail from Jan Beerblock, *The Wards at St John's Hospital, c.* 1778.

Serving a meal, detail from Jan Beerblock, *The Wards at St John's Hospital, c.* 1778.

Nun's chest, Bruges, 17th century. The sisters brought a bridal chest with them on entering the convent. It was used to store their personal belongings.

The religious community

The lay community was transformed in 1459 into a monastic
order that lived according to the
Rule of St Augustine, but which had
no links to other religious houses.
It was subject to the city council

far as practical hospital issues
were concerned, and to the bishop
for religious matters. Candidates
had to complete a trial period last-
ing a year and a day, following
which, provided there were no
impediments, such as a promise of
marriage, debts, disability or contagious disease, they were admitted
into the order. They were chiefly
drawn from among craft and guild
circles – in other words, the then
middle class. Brothers had to be
aged at least 20 to be accepted and
sisters 15. Their habits were white
and black. The brothers dressed
entirely in black, while the sisters
wore a white habit, a black scapular,
a white headscarf and a black cap.
Out of doors, the sisters would also
wear a white hooded cloak. The
hospital's religious community
numbered an average of 20 members at any one time. The male com-

Anonymous, *Triptych with the Holy Trinity,
a Hospital Sister and Patron Saint,* 1551, panel,
64.5 x 43 cm (central panel) and 64.5 x 21.5 cm
(wings) with frame.

Jacob van Oost the Elder (attributed to),
*St Augustine, c.*1660, canvas, 187 x 287 cm.

munity was dissolved in the 16th century, but the number of sisters remained more or less constant until the opening of the new hospital in 1864.

The anonymous *Triptych with the Holy Trinity, a Hospital Sister and Patron Saint* includes hospital sister as patron. She is dressed in her white and black habit. The left wing shows St John the Baptist, while the right one contains Severus, patron saint of weavers, holding a reel. The central panel shows the pilgrim saint, Judocus, presenting the aforementioned hospital sister to the

Holy Trinity – God the Father in heaven, the Holy Spirit in the shape of a dove and Christ, the Son, with his cross and wounds. The water and blood that flow from the wound in his side are collected in a chalice – an image that symbolises Christ's sacrifice as commemorated in the daily celebration of the Eucharist. By commissioning this painting and presenting it to the hospital, the patron, who was probably called Judoca, believed she was contributing to her salvation.

There is a large painting on the south wall of the wards, showing

The Latin Church Father Augustine, who was the patron saint of the religious community at St John's Hospital. The bishop and scholar is shown in his study, working on his book *Confessiones*. The flaming heart, pierced by an arrow, refers to the passage 'You shall pierce our hearts with Your love as with an arrow and Your words shall penetrate our deepest being'.

A legendary episode from Augustine's life is shown in the left background. As he walked along the beach, meditating on the mystery of the Holy Trinity, he saw a child car-rying water from the sea to a small hole. The Church Father explained to the child that its task was impos-sible, to which the child retorted that it was no less impossible for the human mind to fathom the infinite mystery of the Trinity.

Anonymous, *Portrait of Sister Barbara Godtschalk (?–1698) on Her Deathbed*, 1698, canvas, 72 x 107 cm. The deceased sister was Superior of the convent from 1692 until her death.

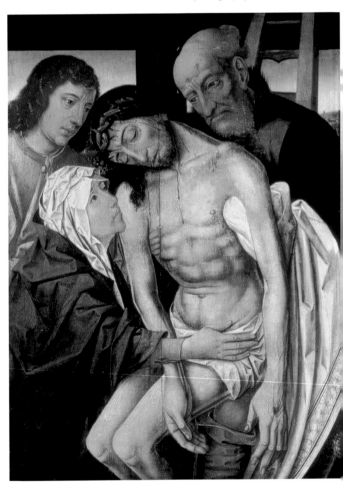

Descent from the Cross, replica of a lost work by Rogier van der Weyden, 15th century, panel, 84.8 x 64 cm. The group, comprising the dead Christ grieved over by those closest to him, is shown in extreme close-up. In this way, Jesus' suffering and death became an almost tangible reality for the worshippers who kneeled before the painting to pray.

Care of the sick and care of the soul

The primary function of the hospital was not to provide medical care. Throughout the first centuries of its existence, it offered shelter and food for the destitute and, if necessary, tended to their injuries. People with contagious diseases were turned away. Care of the sick took a chiefly spiritual form. The most important thing was care of the soul, through daily worship, veneration of the saints, prayer and the sacraments, such as confession, communion and the last rites. The hospital church was actually part of the wards. The hospital did not have its own physician until 1600, but it did have a priest, as the site was a parish in its own right.

Medical treatment did not amount to much. Diagnosis was based on urine examination and astrology, and medicinal herbs were prescribed as a remedy. Things began to improve a little in the 17th century, when greater attention began to be paid to anatomy, direct observation and hygiene. The hospital took on two full-time, university-trained doctors. One noteworthy figure was Thomas Montanus (Van den Berghe), who studied at Louvain University and was associated with the hospital from 1656 until his death in 1685. In 1662, he founded the Guild of St Luke, in order to protect the profession of physician against quacks. Montanus also published a study of the plague, based on his experiences during a major epidemic in Bruges in 1666.

More run-of-the-mill treatments were administered by craft-trained surgeons, who took account of the position of the stars and planets and consulted almanacs, which set out the most auspicious days to perform specific procedures. Barbers bled patients and trimmed their hair and beards. Surgeons and barbers both belonged to the Confraternity of Saints Cosmas and Damian.

Virgin beneath a Canopy, Brussels, 1500–10, gilded and painted wood.

Guilds and confraternities were abolished after the French Revolution. In 1806, a school was set up at St John's Hospital to train 'officiers de santé' (surgeons). Training lasted one year and the school continued until 1835. After that date, medical training was provided solely by the universities. Only now did medical science begin to make genuine progress.

The Visitation, Northern France or Flanders, workshop of the Master of the Rimini Altarpiece, 1430–40, alabaster. The joyful meeting between the pregnant Mary and her cousin Elizabeth, who is also pregnant, is expressively rendered. The decorative and abundant drapery of the robes is also characteristic of this workshop's style.

Religious thinking in the late Middle Ages focused very strongly on suffering and death. Christians hoped that by leading a pious life, they would earn eternal salvation. This attitude is attractively illustrated by the *Diptych of a Franciscan Friar* painted by Jan Provoost (*c.* 1465–1529), an important 16th-century master, who brought new life to painting in Bruges.

The left wing has Christ Carrying the Cross, and the right the portrait of a 54-year-old Franciscan. The rear of the right wing shows a *Memento mori*, while that on the left is painted in imitation red and black stone. The left-hand panel contains a close-up of Christ's upper body, as if the artist had pushed to the front of the crowd to produce it. Three ugly and grimacing faces loom up menacingly behind him, above and to the right. In the upper left corner, we make out part of the faces of the Virgin Mary and St John, whose gentle and sorrowful gaze matches that of Jesus. Their identification with his suffering is strikingly expressed by the similarity between their tears and the drops of blood running down Christ's face. The panel invites the viewer to empathise with Jesus' pain.

The rear of the right panel

features a skull in a niche. The frame, meanwhile, contains a visual puzzle or rebus, which might be interpreted as follows: 'dur est la pensée de la mort – bon est de penser à mi [moi]' (it is hard to think

Jan Provoost, *Diptych of a Franciscan Friar*, 1522, each panel 50 x 40 cm with frame.

of death – it is good to think of me). Interpreted this way, the image is an appeal to meditate on death and Christ. It is not known how the diptych came to be in the hospital collection.

Doctor at a patient's bedside, detail from
Jan Beerblock, *The Wards at St John's Hospital,*
c. 1778.

Anonymous, *Portrait of Franciscus de Wulf,*
early 18th century, canvas, 100 x 78 cm.
Franciscus de Wulf was dean of the Bruges
Surgeons' Guild from 1709 to 1712. He was
famous for his treatment of cataracts.

The charitable work of the hospital sisters
was described in a poetic tribute
written in 1803 to mark the appointment
of a new Superior:

Where the daily work is to feed the hungry,
To give drink to the thirsty and rest to the stranger.
To clothe the naked and, above all, to help
the sick, and to comfort them in great number.

Where so many have been laid to rest!
House of Charity, admired in every town!
Soldier and Protestant, the dissolute, wicked person
Dies here well prepared, comforted as the Lord wishes!

Oh happy house, full of Christian acts,
A true storehouse for all those who are burdened!
Where the wretched shall always find consolation,
Where all is done for God and for salvation's sake.

Jan Beerblock, *The Wards at St John's Hospital, c.* 1778,
canvas, 82 x 153 cm. The Bruges artist Jan Beerblock (1739–1806)
created a lively and realistic portrait of hospital life in 1778.

Horn Reliquary of St Cornelius, Bruges, 16th
century, ivory, silver and silver-gilt. The middle
of the horn contains a relic of Pope Cornelius,
beneath a small silver figure of the saint.
Cornelius' attribute – the horn – relates to
his name ('cornu' is Latin for 'horn'). He was
invoked as a protector against childhood ill-
nesses, fits, cramps and ailments of the head.
He was also the patron saint of horned cattle.
Numerous saints were venerated at St John's
Hospital. Worship of this kind generally
centred on an image of the saint or a relic
(part of the saint's body).

Spending time in hospital

People who could not get to hospital unaided were brought in a litter. They were admitted by a hospital brother who drew up a list of the person's possessions to ensure that he or she was sufficiently poor, and then assessed the patient's condition. It helped to have a recommendation from the parish priest and

Store-cupboard, Flanders, 17th century, oak. Cupboards like this were used to store food. The characteristic, openwork panels consist of interwoven bars, fixed in place with brass rivets. There are both wall-mounted and free-standing versions. The standing ones have a folding plinth underneath. Like the chests used by the hospital sisters, they are pieces of functional rather than decorative furniture.

it was vital to go to confession regularly.

The wards contained rows of wooden beds on either side of the pillars. Each row was a separate department, with its own customs and rights. There were rows for men and women, a surgeon's row and a 'death corner' for terminal cases. The hospital had around a hundred beds in the 18th century, each of which had a straw mattress, linen sheets, woollen blankets and a pillow. There were also several beds in

Hospital activities, details from Jan Beerblock, *The Wards at St John's Hospital, c.* 1778.

he corridors. Known as 'bastard
eds', these were used for patients
equiring intensive care.

The wards were not heated and
were lit with oil-lamps. Nursing
are, meals, visits, prayer and death
ll occurred in the same space, with
very little privacy. Fixed visiting
ours were only introduced in 1762.

An image of the Good Samaritan – the compassionate figure from one of Jesus' parables – will have set the perfect example for the hospital brothers and sisters. The Southern Netherlandish painter Lanceloot Blondeel (1498–1561), to whom the panel has been attributed, came to Bruges at an early age. He was an important figure in the first generation of Renaissance painters in the city.

Several scenes from the parable are depicted in the landscape. On the left, behind the tree, we see a man being attacked by thieves. Several passers-by leave the victim to his fate. The principal episode – the Samaritan tending to the injured man – can be seen in the foreground. On the right, the Samaritan leads the man to an inn and pays the innkeeper. The finely executed landscape and the three-dimensional figures make this a lively and fascinating composition.

Lanceloot Blondeel (attributed to),
The Good Samaritan, second half
16th century, panel, 100.3 x 70.7 cm.

Little evidence is available to tell us how many people died at the hospital. Until the 19th century, however, there was a great deal of ignorance in the fields of medicine, nursing, hygiene and nutrition, and so morality rates in the preceding centuries will undoubtedly have been high. Hospitals served more as refuges than as medical centres, providing the poor and the needy with humane accommodation and the sick with a dignified, religious death. Sick and injured strangers were taken in 'so that they would not die helplessly and wanting in the street'.

'Burying the dead' is one of the seven Acts of Mercy. This task, too, was performed by the community of St John's Hospital, more specifically by the chaplain and a servant. There was a cemetery on the site, which was not only used to bury people who died at the hospital itself, but also served as the last resting place of those executed at the city prison and of all the penniless dead found in Bruges. Sisters, brothers and chaplains were interred in the church. Burials on the hospital grounds came to an end around 1800.

Religious care of the dying, details from Jan Beerblock, *The Wards at St John's Hospital,* c. 1778. One of the rows of beds in the wards was known as the 'death corner'.

St Cornelius, Bruges, late 14th century, gilded and painted oak. This statue is the most important 14th-century wooden sculpture in Bruges. It has always been at St John's Hospital, where Cornelius was one of a group of saints venerated in their capacity as 'healers'. The horn (*cornu* in Latin) refers to the name of this early Pope.

The church in the north aisle forms part of the wards. The Chapel of St Cornelius was built onto the church in the 14th century. The three wards and the church belonged to a single space until the beginning of the 19th century, when they were split up into different sections. The original configuration has now largely been restored.

You enter the church through the door that used to close off the Chapel of St Cornelius. Cornelius himself is enthroned above the entrance. You will, of course, be eager to see the Memlings, but while you are here, be sure to take a look at the interior of the church, as this reflects the hospital's long history and contains a lot of interesting items.

The tabernacles on the wall (used to store hosts that have been blessed for use during the Eucharist) and the four niches date from the Middle Ages. The large sandstone tabernacle on the wall of the choir was installed in 1477, while the one in the Chapel of St Cornelius is older (*c*. 1410–20). Both are fine examples of small-scale, late-Gothic architecture. Memling's *St John Altarpiece* adorned the high altar in the late 15th century. His *St Ursula Shrine* was also displayed in the church. It was kept in a painted chest on ordinary days, but was revealed in all its glory on feast days. The statue of St Cornelius stood on the altar of the side-chapel.

The decorative brass candleholder in the Chapel of St Cornelius is a piece of early 16th-century work.

The church was refurbished in the Baroque style in the 17th century. A new altar deserves a new altarpiece, and so Memling's *St John Altarpiece* was replaced in 1637 by Jacob Van Oost the Elder's *Virgin and Saints*. The choir-stalls, which date from 1661, comprise two lots of five seats and are abundantly decorated with putti, caryatids in elegant robes, holy figures, the Gospel writers, and so on. The confessional is surmounted with a medallion containing the hospital's emblem – the poisoned chalice and lamb. The two doorways – the former door from the Chapel of St Cornelius and the luxuriantly carved Appolonia doorway – date from the Baroque period. The latter now closes off the Chapel of St Cornelius, but originally belonged to the Chapel of St Appolonia, which was constructed against the façade on Mariastraat.

The wrought-iron, Louis-XIV-style communion rail was added to the choir in the late 18th century. The brass medallions (1792) show a number of figures, including Saints John the Baptist, John the Evangelist, Augustine and Ursula. The silversmith Gaspard Hanicq made them after a design by Jan Beerblock, who also painted *The Wards at St John's Hospital.*

The church was extended over part of the wards in the 19th century. The two rood lofts and the organ above them were installed at that time.

Of the six masterpieces by Hans Memling that can be seen in the church and in the Chapel of St Cornelius, four were painted for the hospital and have remained there ever since. St John's Hospital was an important Bruges institution in Memling's time, and having a large painting by the celebrated artist on the high altar of its church further enhanced the prestige of the hospital community.

Hans Memling is first mentioned in a document dated to January 1465, when he registered as a citizen of Bruges. His entry in the citizen's register gives his name as Jan van Mimnelinghe and states that he was born in the German town of Seligenstadt on the river Main. As time passed, he appears to have modified his name to Hans Memling, as he is frequently identified in Bruges documents as 'Meester Hans' and he signed two of his works – the St John Altarpiece and the Triptych of Jan Floreins, both of which can be seen in St John's Hospital – with the name 'Memling'. His father or grandfather probably came from Mömlingen, a village located on a tributary of the Main called the Mömling, 5 km to the south of Seligenstadt.

Memling is believed to have been about 25 when he came to Bruges as a fully trained painter. Nothing is known of his childhood, but art historians believe that he trained in Cologne and then spent time as an assistant at Rogier van der Weyden's workshop in Brussels. This view is borne out by the similarity of his work with that of contemporary Cologne painters and Van der Weyden. There is also the coincidence of his arrival in Bruges shortly after Rogier's death.

It did not take long for him to start receiving prestigious commissions. Memling became the favoured artist of the bourgeois elite, the senior clergy and Bruges' foreign merchant community. Within the space of a few years, he became one of the city's wealthiest citizens. In 1473–74, he joined the religious confraternity of Our Lady of the Snows – an elite group attached to the church of Our Lady, opposite St John's Hospital.

It was around this time that Memling started work on the Triptych of John the Baptist and John the Evangelist (the St John Altarpiece) for the church at St John's Hospital. He completed the altarpiece in 1479. That same year, and the one after, the artist also supplied two smaller triptychs for the hospital or the attached monastery – the Triptych of Jan Floreins and the Triptych

of Adriaan Reins. The Portrait of a Young Woman and the Diptych of Maarten van Nieuwenhove, which were presented to St John's Hospital in the 19th century, were painted in the 1480s. The St Ursula Shrine was installed in the hospital church in 1489.

Memling lived with his wife Tanne (Anna de Valkenaere) and their three children, Hannekin, Neelkin and Claykin, in a large brick house on Sint-Jorisstraat, where he ran his workshop. This will have employed a variety of assistants to help him grind pigments and mix paint, prepare the panels, apply the basic layers of colour and embellish his landscapes. Memling was, after all, a highly productive painter – especially during the peak of his career in the 1480s.

He died in Bruges on 11 August 1494, prompting a contemporary to note in his diary that the 'most gifted and excellent master in all Christendom' had passed away.

Triptych of St John the Baptist and St John the Evangelist, detail from the right wing (see p. 37).
Memling's paintings present an ideal Christian universe, in which mortals and holy figures come together mystically. Yet they also reflect the real world, more specifically that of wealthy, late-medieval Bruges.

Triptych of St John the Baptist and St John the Evangelist 1474–79

Hans Memling c. 1440–1494
Panel, 173.5 x 173.5 cm (central panel), 176 x 79 cm (wings)
Altarpiece for the high altar of the church at St John's Hospital, Bruges
(central panel) *Virgin and Child Enthroned with Four Saints*
(wings) *The Beheading of St John the Baptist* (left)
and *The Apocalypse of St John the Evangelist*
(exterior) *Jacob de Ceuninc and Antheunis Seghers with their Patron Saints* (left)
and *Agnes Casembrood and Clara van Hulsen with their Patron Saints*

Open triptych

Four senior clerics at St John's Hospital commissioned this altarpiece for their church, probably to mark the completion of the new apse in 1473–74. They had themselves immortalised on the rear of the two wings, which meant that on ordinary weekdays, when the triptych was closed, all that could be seen was these four praying figures and their patron saints. The shutters were opened on Sundays and feast days, allowing the hospital's residents to admire the painting in all its glory.

The original inscription at the bottom of the frame reads OPUS IOHANNIS MEMLING ANNO M CCCC LXXIX 1479 (the work of Johannes Memling in the year 1479).

The central panel shows the Virgin Mary as Queen of Heaven, sitting on her throne with the Christ Child. The elegant women at her feet are Catharine and Barbara, two popular medieval saints, behind whom stand John the Baptist and John the Evangelist, the hospital's two patrons.

Catharine can be identified from the wheel on which, according to her legend, she was tortured, and the sword with which she was beheaded. Her 'mystic marriage' with Christ, which she saw in a vision, is also represented here in the way the Child slips a ring onto her finger. The theme is apt, in that the two female donors were nuns and hence 'brides of Christ'.

The legend of St Barbara also refers to monastic life. She spent her days in isolation and prayer, having been imprisoned in a tower by her heathen father, who eventually murdered her because of her piety. Barbara was invoked against sudden death, without the sacraments of confession or communion – a fate that frequently threatened the residents of a home for the sick and destitute.

According to the Bible, John the Baptist was Christ's cousin and forerunner. He was beheaded on the orders of King Herod. The lamb at his side alludes to what he said about Jesus – 'Ecce Agnus Dei' (Behold, the Lamb of God). The other St John – the Evangelist – was one of Christ's apostles and the author of one of the four Gospels and the *Book of Revelation*. He holds a goblet in his hand, recalling the

Closed triptych

poisoned chalice from which he had to drink as a test of his faith.

The group is shown in a loggia, beyond which extends a landscape with ruins and the buildings of a town. The capitals of the marble columns, the landscape in the background and the wings of the altarpiece all feature numerous episodes from the legends of the two St Johns. Those on the left relate to John the Baptist and those on the right to John the Evangelist.

The left half of the central panel includes the Baptist preaching in the wilderness, his arrest and the burning of his decapitated body. The most important little scenes in the left wing are the Baptism of Christ in the Jordan – in the far distance, with God looking down from the clouds – and Salome's dance in Herod's palace. As a reward for her

Detail from the central panel

39

performance, Salome demanded John's head. The beheading takes place in the yard in front of a grim prison tower.

The other half of the central panel and the right wing of the altarpiece are devoted to St John the Evangelist. On the first capital next to the canopy, he is shown drinking from the poisoned chalice, while between the two clustered pillars on the right, we see him immersed in boiling oil. Having survived these torments unscathed, he was eventually banished. Further in the background, he can be made out as he boards the boat that will take him to the island of Patmos, where he was to have his vision of the End of the World.

The whole of the right wing is given over to the *Apocalypse.* John himself sits in the foreground, with his book, pen and inkpot. Hans Memling depicts the key passages from the Bible text very precisely. God appears in the middle of the concentric rainbows, holding in his right hand a book with seven seals, which is also being clasped by a lamb with seven horns and seven eyes. An angel stands on the edge of the rainbow, pointing to the book and asking John: 'Who is worthy to open the scroll and break its seals?' The lamb breaks six of them, prompting the appearance of four horsemen. Cosmic catastrophes, including an eclipse and falling stars, afflict the earth. 'When the Lamb opened the seventh seal, there was silence in heaven for about half an hour...' Seven angels with trumpets then unleash another series of terrible scourges. An eagle soars in the sky, calling out: 'Woe! Woe! Woe to the inhabitants of the earth, at the blasts of the other trumpets that the three angels are about to blow!' Finally, the Virgin Mary appears high in the sky on a crescent moon. She is dressed with the sun and wears a crown

Details from the left panel

with twelve stars, and is threatened by the dragon, while her Child is borne up to heaven by an angel. The dragon is defeated by the Archangel Michael. On the horizon, however, the seven-headed, blasphemous Beast rises out of the sea: 'And the dragon gave it its power and his throne and great authority.'

Memling conveys this hallucinatory dream in a single, undivided painting, turning it into a coherent composition in which all the elements interlock. He also made a great effort to render the theme realistically, as we see in the reflections in the sea and the way he represents the musical instruments.

The *St John Altarpiece* unites three aspects of the Christian universe – heaven, which is timeless, human history, with its cruelty and sin, and the future, which holds the End of the World, which the wicked must fear and the righteous must long for. The peaceful gathering of the holy company offered pious worshippers a glimpse of the bliss, free of illness and pain, that awaited them in the hereafter.

Details from the right panel

Fifteenth-century Flanders was a prosperous region ruled by the splendour-loving Burgundian dynasty. Peace, wealth and civilised refinement provided an excellent climate for the development of art. Bruges, Ghent, Brussels and Louvain were all home to artists whose work is amongst the most valuable ever created by humanity. They were able to develop their talent in an ideal manner thanks to the patronage of the aristocracy, wealthy burghers and the Church. These painters have been dubbed the Flemish Primitives ('primitive' referring to the earliest form of painting on wooden panels or on canvas in the Low Countries). Hans Memling was one of them.

Details from the central panel

To the right of the cloth of honour, Memling depicts the Kraanplaats in Bruges. Brothers from St John's Hospital are shown in front of the large wooden crane from which the square took its name. They are inspecting barrels of wine from Bordeaux – a lucrative privilege bestowed on them by the city council.

Hans Memling c. 1440–1494
Panel, 46.3 x 57.4 cm (central panel), 48.3 x 25 cm (wings)
(central panel) *The Adoration of the Magi*
(wings) *The Nativity* (left) and *The Presentation in the Temple*
(exterior) *John the Baptist* (left) and *St Veronica*

According to Memling's own inscription on the frame, this painting was commissioned from him by Brother Jan Floreins, also known as Vander Rijst, a brother at St John's Hospital in Bruges, in 1479. The 36-year-old Floreins (his age is inscribed in the stonework alongside his head) had himself included discreetly in the central panel, kneeling in prayer behind a low wall. Perhaps he is reading the passage in the gospel in which the visit of the Wise Men is described. Deep in pious meditation, the sacred events appear before him as in a vision.

The Virgin Mary sits in a dilapidated stable with the Infant Christ on her lap. Her husband, Joseph, stands at her side, but holds himself somewhat in the background. The Three Kings – actually three philosophers from the East – treat the Child with immense respect and offer him gold, frankincense and myrrh. The stable contains the traditional ox and ass, symbolising the Jews and the heathens. The ox is bound by the law – a rope is tied around its horns. The ass, meanwhile, bows its head under the weight of idolatry. There are several secondary characters in the middle-ground who do not feature in the story as recounted in the Bible – the young man behind Jan Floreins, the man with the cap who peers in through the window on the right and

Open triptych

the little boy on the far right, whom we glimpse behind the arm of the elegant Moorish king. These are all probably portraits.

As was customary with the Flemish Primitives, the biblical story is given a medieval Flemish setting – a picturesque city view in a rolling, green landscape. A group of

...iders, including one on a camel, ...nd several other intriguing figures ...make their way from the town ...owards the stable. The ruins – the ...table itself and the frontmost ...uilding in the background – sym-...olise the downfall of heathendom ...n the coming of the Redeemer.

The left wing shows the Nativity of Christ, while the one on the right features the Presentation in the Temple. Memling does not, how-ever, place the latter in a temple but in a more familiar context, namely Bruges' Romanesque Cathedral of St Donatian, which no longer exists. We can make out a city square through the open door. In this way,

Closed triptych

Memling used the characteristic painting techniques of artists in 15th-century Flanders. The Flemish Primitives perfected the technique of painting in oil on oak panels. They began with a white ground layer, on which transparent colours were placed in a series of thin layers. The result was an unmatched brightness and colours that continue to gleam, many centuries later. The combination of this technique and their acute observation of reality enabled them to achieve an exquisitely refined representation of the physical world. Their realism paralleled the religious interpretation of the cosmos as God's creation, taking in both heaven and earth. Consequently, their paintings are also full of symbolism. The art of the Flemish Primitives is viewed at once as a final manifestation of the late-Gothic style and as the first appearance of the Renaissance in northern painting.

the artist brings the sacred events as close as possible to the viewer. It is as if Mary, the prophetess Anne and the elderly Simeon were presenting the Child to the Bruges congregation.

There are two marvellous saints' images on the rear of the wings. Through a richly carved archway, we look onto a deep landscape with John the Baptist in the left foreground and St Veronica, with her cloth bearing the image of Christ's face, on the right. The panorama with its wide river and rocky outcrops runs continuously across the two panels. The one on the left evokes the Holy Land by placing the Baptism of Christ on the river bank. The frames still have their original imitation marble painting, in which the patron's initials, IF, are incorporated three times, together with his coats of arms. The altarpiece's lock – also original – is an interesting example of 15th-century wrought-iron work.

Memling based this small devotional painting on earlier compositions by Rogier van der Weyden. However, he took his predecessor's influence and applied it in his own way, producing a work in his characteristically restrained and slightly sweet style. Typical features include Joseph's tender gaze and the joyful gesture of Mary and the angels in the Nativity, and narrative elements such as Joseph taking two turtle-doves from a basket as a gift for the temple.

The panel was framed before the artist began to work on the painting, and the frame was painted before the panels it contains were finished. This is apparent, for instance, from the way part of the robe worn by the king kneeling at Mary's knee is painted over the bottom of the frame. Memling used trompe-l'oeil touches like this to reduce the distance between the imaginary space of the painter and the real world of the viewer.

Details from the central panel

The Virgin Mary is shown with her child in a Bruges parlour, circa 1487. The open window looks out over a Flemish landscape. Maarten van Nieuwenhove sits in the same room. The inscription tells us that he had his portrait painted at the age of 23 in 1487. The window behind him overlooks the bridge across the Minnewater.

The serene and regal Madonna forms a triangle inscribed within the rectangle of the panel, a device through which Memling turns her into a stylised image – an icon. She answers the idea of beauty that we find throughout his oeuvre.

The patron is also presented in an idealised yet life-like way. Maarten van Nieuwenhove was a prominent citizen of Bruges. His confident pose, velvet jerkin and robe, trimmed with black fur, testify to his power and wealth. He is accompanied in the customary way by his patron saint, whom we make out in the stained-glass window in the upper right of the painting. St Martin is shown cutting his cloak in two, so that he can give half to a beggar.

Over the centuries, the underdrawing in the right-hand panel has gradually begun to show through the thin layers of paint. This helps us to reconstruct Memling's working methods. He generally sketched the entire composition on the white preparatory layer applied to the wooden panel. His drawing style is searching and energetic, with corrections in the outlines and poses, as we see, for instance, in the hands and sleeves. The style of the underdrawing thus differs markedly from the sharply outlined and static finished product.

In the most distant window in this panel, a number of construction lines for the wall and windows show through the paint layers. These tell us something about the complex structure of a painting of this nature, and also show how Memling used trial and error to achieve the correct representation of depth.

Maarten van Nieuwenhove sits with the Virgin Mary in a logically constructed interior. The viewer looks at them both as if through two windows – the configuration is reflected in the convex mirror above the Virgin's right shoulder. The artist sought to create the illusion that the framed panel was an open

AN · VERO·ETATIS· SVE ·: 23 ·

...indow with a view of a real, three-
...imensional world, with ideal
...eople and landscapes.

Painting in the 15th century was largely religious in inspiration. The most common themes were scenes set in heaven or from the life of Christ, his mother Mary, and the saints and martyrs. The patrons were also incorporated in this pious context. They had their portraits painted in the company of their patron saints or kneeling before the Virgin. Paintings of this kind were presented to churches, where they adorned altars or chapels. Sometimes, they were used by the patron for private worship, in which case they were installed in his or her home.

Contemplation of these images encouraged worshippers to pray, meditate and emulate the example of Christ and the saints. The presentation of the invisible as part of a tangible world reinforced the links between the divine and everyday, and brought people closer to God and to eternal life.

St Ursula Shrine before 1489

Hans Memling *c.* 1440–1494
Mainly oak, gilded and painted carvings
and painted panels, 91.5 x 99 x 41.5 cm

Ursula was a devout Breton princess, whom a heathen prince, son of the King of England, wished to marry. She agreed, on condition that he converted to Christianity and that she be allowed to make a pilgrimage to Rome, accompanied by 11,000 virgins. Eutherius did not object and so Ursula travelled by boat and on foot via Cologne and Basle to Rome, where her immense company was received by the Pope. During the return journey, she was captured by Guam, King of the Huns, in Cologne. His soldiers murdered Ursula, her betrothed, Eutherius, the 11,000 virgins and the Pope and his retinue, who had accompanied them on their way. Ursula's story came from the *Legenda Aurea* – a collection of saints' lives, compiled in the 13th century by Jacob de Voragine. The 'Golden Legend' was the standard source in the Middle Ages for the lives of the saints and martyrs.

Hans Memling made the *St Ursula Shrine* for the religious community at St John's Hospital, for which Ursula was the focus of special veneration. An important ceremony took place in the hospital church on 21 October 1489, the saint's feast day, when Ursula's relics were transferred from the old shrine, which is also still to be seen in the hospital, and placed in Memling's *St Ursula Shrine.* The artist himself may well have been present, together with many other prominent guests. Jan Floreins, who commissioned the small triptych that includes his portrait, was

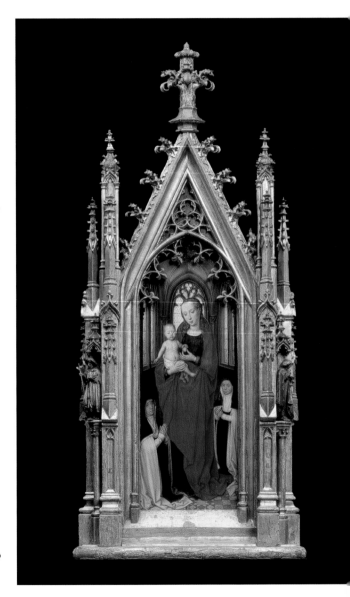

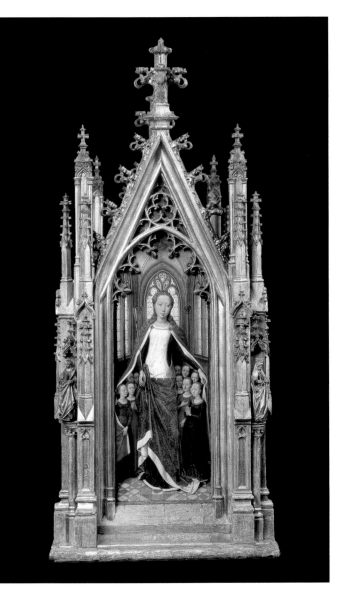

Master at the time. Jacob de Ceuninc, who is included as one of the donors in the left wing of the *St John Altarpiece,* was also one of the community's administrators in 1489, serving as bursar.

The wooden relic-chest is shaped like a chapel with a saddle roof. The paintings are like stained-glass windows. One narrow end is decorated with a Virgin and Child in a Gothic choir, with two kneeling hospital sisters at her side. The other end has St Ursula in a similar setting, with an arrow in her right hand. Ten virgins huddle beneath her cloak.

The story of Ursula's pilgrimage is recounted in six scenes, three on each of the long sides. Each scene incorporates several episodes from the legend.

The story begins with the first stop on the Rhine at Cologne. Memling leaves out the background story with the marriage proposal, the assembly of the 11,000 virgins and so on.

The overall work is unbelievably detailed and subtly conceived. The Cologne cityscapes are especially realistic (Memling himself must have spent time in Cologne), as are the boats, the plants, the costumes and the armour, in which the bystanders are reflected.

The shrine was kept in the hospital church in a painted wooden chest
from which it was only removed on feast days, including that of St Ursula.

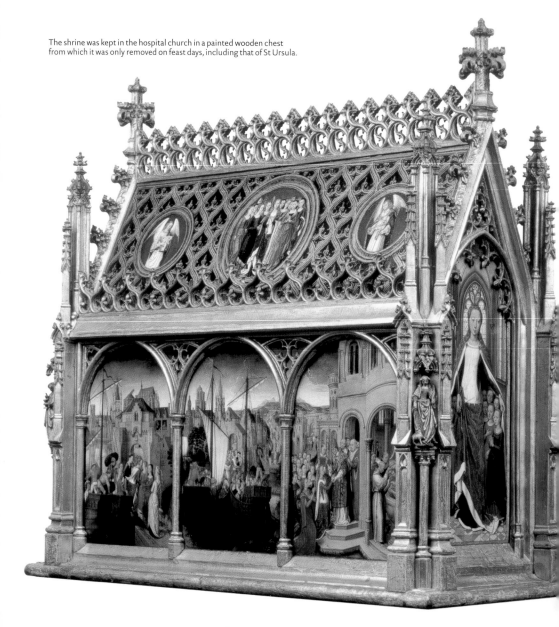

St James of Compostella.

Musician Angels, medallions on the roof.

Arrival in Cologne. The company spends the night in the city. An angel warns Ursula of her impending martyrdom.

Departure from Basle. The Pope and his retinue accompany the pilgrims.

The martyrdom on arrival in Cologne. The Huns attack and kill the pilgrims. Eutherius is stabbed to death in Ursula's arms.

Arrival in Basle. The group continues its journey across the mountains.

Arrival in Rome. The pilgrims, with Ursula and Eutherius at their head, are welcomed by Pope Cyriacus and receive the sacraments: Eutherius makes his confession, Ursula is given communion and baptisms are performed.

The martyrdom of Ursula. She rejects the advances of the Hun leader and is shot with an arrow.

Hans Memling c. 1440–1494
Panel, 43.8 x 35.8 cm (central panel), 45.3 x 14.3 cm (wings)
(central panel) *The Lamentation over Christ*
(wings) *Adriaan Reins with St Adriaan* (left) and *St Barbara*
(closed shutters) *St Wilgefortis* (left) and *St Mary of Egypt*

Shortly after Jan Floreins had commissioned his little triptych from Hans Memling, another hospital brother, Adriaan Reins, decided to follow his example. The principal theme in this case is the Lamentation on Golgotha. Jesus' body has just been lowered from the cross and his mother kneels alongside it in prayer. Christ's most beloved disciple, St John, gently removes the crown of thorns. A distraught Mary Magdalene sits behind Jesus' mother. The three figures are overwhelmed with grief – tears flow down their faces. In the distance, Nicodemus and Joseph of Arimathea prepare the tomb. As with the *Floreins Triptych*, Memling took a painting by Rogier van der Weyden as his basis – Mary Magdalene's grief-stricken pose, for instance, is typical of the Brussels master. The high, luminous horizon gives the scene a very enclosed, even intimate atmosphere. Jerusalem is picked out against it, beneath a lowering evening sky. The outline of another city can also be made out in the hazy, blue distance. The landscape runs across three panels, unifying the overall image.

Adriaan Reins' initials are painted at the bottom of the frame in imitation gold letters, while the year '1480' is inscribed at the top. Brother Adriaan is shown kneeling in the left wing, accompanied by his patron saint, Adrian, who was a warrior from the early Christian period. The saint holds a hammer and an anvil, the instruments of his martyrdom. The lion at his feet is a symbol of his courage. Adrian was invoked against the plague – Bruges fell victim to the Black Death

repeatedly in the 15th century. The right wing contains the figure of St Barbara, who was believed to protect her devotees from sudden death without receiving the final sacraments.

Two elegant female saints appear on the rear of the wings. According to her legend, Wilgefortis was a

ious princess, who miraculously grew a beard to enable her to escape an arranged marriage with a heathen prince, following which defiance, she was crucified by her own father. Like Barbara, she was invoked as a protectress of the dying, which explains her nickname 'Uncumber' – those who invoked her in their final hour could die unencumbered with anxiety. The other shutter has an image of the repentant sinner, St Mary of Egypt, who lived forty years in the wilderness sustained only by three loaves of bread. She was sometimes confused with Mary Magdalene, who was also a penitent.

Open triptych

Details from the left and right panels

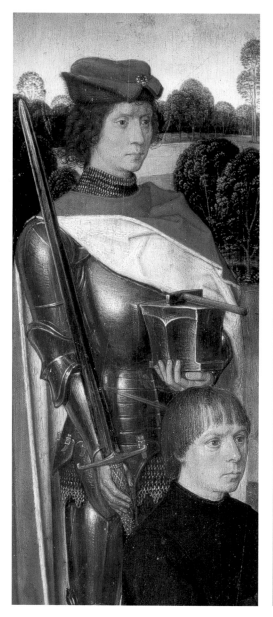

Memling's style is highly dis-
tinctive. Idealised, slender
figures come together in
paradisaical surroundings.
The composition is balanced,
the execution flawless and
the mood a touch sentimen-
tal. Memling offered his own
personal synthesis of the
innovations of his great pre-
decessors, Jan van Eyck and
Rogier van der Weyden.
From the very beginning, he
shared their focus on colour
and light, the painstakingly
detailed rendering of materials and objects, and the
importance placed on the
landscape element. He bor-
rowed many compositions
and poses from Rogier, not to
mention his probable mas-
ter's sublime portrait technique. He was highly skilled
at integrating figures and
groups in their surroundings
and he also worked hard to
achieve convincing perspec-
tive. Deep landscapes and
precise townscapes unfold
with endless fascination in
the distance behind his eleg-
antly dressed figures.

is plain from this young woman's
clothes and jewellery that she
belonged to Bruges' wealthy bour-
geoisie. Memling painted the portrait of a contemporary and not that
of a classical literary figure, the
Sibylla Sambetha, as the inscription
suggests. The disfiguring cartouche
was inserted in the first half of the
16th century, as was the text on the
streamer at the bottom of the frame.
The streamer itself and the year
'1480' are, however, authentic.

Memling's simultaneously realistic yet idealising style made him a
highly sought-after portraitist. He
gave his sitters' faces a soft, purified
form, with very little shadow or
contrast.

The woman appears to be sitting
at an open window. Her fingertips
rest on the frame, creating the
impression that she is looking out of
her imaginary world into the real
space occupied by the viewer. This
sense of proximity, the dreamy
expression and the simple, yet stylish clothing and jewellery heighten
the fascination of this image of an
unidentified woman.

THE ATTICS

Cross-section of the roof construction in the central attic.

1   Parapet
2   Sole piece
3   Socle
4   Ashlar post
5   Rafter
6   Curved brace
7   Wooden grate
8   Collar
9   Purlin
10 Roof post

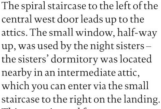

The spiral staircase to the left of the central west door leads up to the attics. The small window, half-way up, was used by the night sisters – the sisters' dormitory was located nearby in an intermediate attic, which you can enter via the small staircase to the right on the landing. This room is used for temporary exhibitions.

Only the first two bays (the first two sections of the room), beginning at the west wall, made up the sisters' dormitory. You can see a fragment of the 14th-century floor and remains of a fireplace – one of the oldest hearths in Bruges. If you look out of the windows, you can see the stylish 19th-century hospital buildings on the right and the convent on the left.

Your tour of the museum now takes you through the central attic with its imposing oak beams, dating from the late 13th century. The roof supports are constructed in the form of a barrel vault, with large, curved braces and a fascinating pattern of structural elements above and between them. At the very back, against the east wall, is a model of the tympanum of the Virgin Mary Porch.

The attics not only served as the hospital's roof space. The ventilation of the wards, which will have been filled with unhealthy vapours and stench, also occurred via this space. Air flowed out through wooden grates in the ceiling – an example of a ventilation grate of this kind can still be seen in the reception area, roughly in the middle of the ceiling.

Running water and decent ventilation were crucial to hygiene within the hospital. Not only did the Reie wash away waste and dirt, the atmospheric turbulence it generated also helped clean the lowest layers of air. The contaminated, evil-smelling air in the wards was drawn up by this natural ventilation process into the attic and then outside.

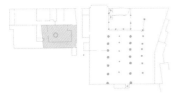

The cloister

You pass through the cloister, with its atmospheric garden, on your way to the pharmacy, the Governors' Chamber and the Chaplain's Room. In addition to a few chests, in which the sisters kept their meagre possessions and clothes, and store cupboards for food, you can see a 15th-century Calvary group here. Also note the asymmetrical roof trusses.

The monastery gate in the hospital grounds.

The 16th-century cloister of the former monastery.

Box for storing resin, 17th century, painted wood.

The pharmacy

In 1643, a member of the Herbalists' Guild in Bruges was asked to set up a pharmacy in the former monastery of St John's Hospital. The pharmacy was run by a number of sisters, and remained in existence until 1971, complete with its original fixtures and fittings from the 17th, 18th and 19th centuries. It was then incorporated in the museum.

The oak dispensing table, the brown jars in glazed stoneware, and the wooden barrels and chests are 17th century, while most of the remaining furniture and objects are 18th century.

Against the wall at the back stands a herb cupboard, with small drawers in which dried herbs were stored. To the right of this, in a niche with a stained-glass window, is the plaster cupboard, containing small compartments in which rolled-up plasters were placed. 'Plaster' referred at this time to a piece of fabric impregnated with a medicinal ointment. The imposing name of the plaster, or *emplastra,* is painted on each compartment: E. Gracia Dei ('Plaster of the Grace of God' for drying wounds), E. Divinum ('The Divine Plaster', for the treatment of corns) and so forth. The resins and gums with which plasters were prepared were contained in the black boxes on the shelves. Herbal remedies, such as liquorice root and poppyheads, were also stored here.

The boxes and barrels are painted the colour of mahogany, with gilded inscriptions. In the corner next to the plaster cupboard is a wooden cupboard with two full doors and two small, folding doors in the middle. This is the poison cupboard, which could, of course, be well sealed. The small cupboard on top of the elongated piece of furniture midway between the shelves, is the 'simplicia' cupboard. This contained samples of most ingredients or 'simplicia', such as herbs, resins and minerals, which were used to make preparations or 'composita'. The cupboard has eight cardboard drawers with compartments into which the samples were sorted.

There are dozens of pharmacist's pots and bottles on the shelves. The oldest are the brown jars, in which medicinal waters, wines and syrups were stored. The white, glazed earthenware pots with blue labels date from somewhat later. The bottles with wooden stoppers contained herb-water, as indicated by the 'A' (for *aqua*) on the label. The cylindrical pots with tin lids held ointment ('U' for *unguentum*), pills ('P' for *pilulae*) or extracts ('E' for *extractum*). The pots with spouts were used for oil ('O' for *oleum*). The ones with a base, spout, wooden stopper and tin lid held syrup ('S' for *sirupus*). The small wooden pots contained all manner of raw materials. The series of glass bottles dates from the 19th century. The pharmacy also has weighing scales and several mortars, in which ingredients were ground up with heavy pestles.

The pharmacy was simultaneously a laboratory, shop and nursing station for outpatient care.

Delftware pharmacist's pot, 17th century.

Bearded jug, Bouffioulx, first half 17th century, stoneware. Bouffioulx was an important centre for the production of earthenware in the 16th and 17th centuries. Typical decorative elements include the purely ornamental coat of arms, the band patterns and the head from which this type of vessel derives its name.

Philippe van Bree, *The Pharmacy at St John's Hospital*, first half 19th century, panel, 90 x 110 cm. The painting illustrates how the pharmacy operated. On the right, we see a sister sorting herbs, referring to Dodoens' famous herbal. Another sister is grinding ingredients in a large bronze mortar. Two more are preparing medicines behind the imposing dispensing table. A mother sits and waits for a remedy for her sick son. The interior has hardly changed to this day.

Pharmacist's pot, 15th century (?),
glazed and painted earthenware.
(Chaplain's Room)

The Governors' Chamber

This room with its Baroque, oak
furniture used to be the pharmacy's
drawing room. However, since two
series of governors' portraits were
installed here in 1891, it has been
referred to as the 'Governors'
Chamber'. One series – the one with
the inscriptions at the bottom –
shows the governors of St John's
Hospital. The earliest portrait is
that of *Johannes Despars* (1618),
the painter of which is not known.
The series has always been in the
hospital and is almost complete.
The other series shows the governors of St Julian's Hospital – another
Bruges institution, which cared for
the mentally ill and foundlings. The
portraits date from the 16th–18th
century, as St Julian's was closed
down during the region's annexa-
tion by revolutionary France. This
group is less complete than the
other, as a third of the paintings
have been lost. Both series include
some extremely fine old portraits,
most of which will have been
painted by Bruges artists.

The furniture in the Governors'
Chamber includes two interesting
17th-century oak sideboards. One is
decorated with scenes from the
hospital and the pharmacy, and was
made especially for St John's. The
second has animal and plant motifs,
and figures playing musical instruments.

The wooden Christmas cradle produced around 1425–50 is a fascinating religious object from the realm of popular devotion. It is painted and gilded, and has an embroidered blanket made in 1714, with a silver image of the Christ Child. The cradle used to be rocked during church services at Christmas.

Detail of the wall in the Governors' Chamber with Delft-style tiles, late 17th century. A document in the hospital archives records the purchase in 1694 of a batch of tiles illustrated with children's games.

The ward in the 17th century, detail of a sideboard, Bruges, 1678. This piece of decorative oak furniture was made especially for St John's hospital.

Anonymous, *Francisco Pardo, Governor of
St Julian's Hospital*, 1604, panel, 51 x 39 cm.

From the second half of the 13th century, Bruges'
charitable institutions were placed under the
supervision of two governors appointed by the
city council. These individuals usually belonged
to the civic elite. As occurred in other cities, a
small number of influential families monopolised
power in Bruges, especially in the 17th and 18th
centuries. That explains why the same surnames
and coats of arms appear several times among the
governors' portraits. The tradition of governors'
portraits was continued after the French Revolution, although now it was members of the Commission for Civil Almshouses and later Municipal
Social Services who had their portraits painted.
The custom continues to this day.

The Chaplain's Room

Following the closure of the monastery, one of the rooms around the cloister was turned into a sitting room for the hospital chaplain. The room is now used to display pharmacopoeias (pharmaceutical reference books), herbals, a number of containers and other objects that once belonged to the hospital pharmacy.

The corbel pieces are architectural elements from the time of the monastery's construction. The fine oak display case with its window is 18th century and was made especially for the hospital.

orbel piece, *c.* 1460–70.
he angel holds the hospital's
ms with the symbols of
: John the Evangelist and
: John the Baptist – a poisoned
halice and a lamb.

Rembert Dodoens, *Cruydt-Boeck,* title page, Antwerp, 1644. The first edition of the famous herbal by the botanist Dodoens (1517–1585) was published in 1554 and the last in 1644. It describes the different plants, their characteristics and medicinal properties, and how to prepare them.

The Brussels Pharmacopoeia of 1739, frontispiece. A pharmacopoeia was an official book of medicines, in which the usual remedies were set out, together with their composition, properties and preparation instructions.

I am grateful to Dr Valentin Vermeersch, Honorary Curator, and Manfred Sellink, Chief Curator of the Municipal Museums of Bruges, for their interest, and to Hilde Lobelle-Caluwé, Curator of the Memling Museum–St John's Hospital, for her crucial assistance and the unfailingly friendly way in which she offered it.

May Song, 1 May 1828, watercolour on paper, detail. May Songs were sung at the traditional May Day service at St John's Hospital. The words were written by two of the sisters, illustrated with a May tree or branches. The May Song was read out during a festive meal in the refectory and then presented to the Mistress.
(Wards)

Contents

The Death of the Virgin, with Christ and the Apostles, detail from the tympanum of the Virgin Mary Porch, late 13th century.

Hans Memling, *Triptych of St John the Baptist and St John the Evangelist,* detail (see p. 37)

The information in this guide is drawn from several general and specialist publications on the history of Bruges, St John's Hospital Museum and Hans Memling:

800 jaar Sint-Janshospitaal Brugge, exhibition catalogue, Hilde Lobelle-Caluwé (ed.), 2 vols, Bruges 1976.

Hilde Lobelle-Caluwé, *Memling Museum Bruges,* in the series 'Musea Nostra', Ministry of the Flemish Community/Crédit Communal/Ludion, Ghent 1987.

Hilde Lobelle-Caluwé, *Hans Memling, het succes van een kunstenaar,* Openbaar Kunstbezit in Vlaanderen, *s.l.* and *s.d.*

Dirk De Vos, *Hans Memling,* Fonds Mercator, Antwerp 1994.

Dirk De Vos et al., *Hans Memling, Catalogue – Essays,* exhibition catalogue, 2 vols, Bruges 1994.

Na het oude Sint-Jans reeds tien jaar A.Z., published for the exhibition to mark the tenth anniversary of the General Hospital in Bruges, Hilde Lobelle-Caluwé (ed.), Bruges 1987.

Maximiliaan P.J. Martens et al., *Bruges and the Renaissance. From Memling to Pourbus,* exhibition catalogue, Stichting Kunstboek/Ludion, Bruges 1998.

Valentin Vermeersch, *Bruges, A Thousand Years of Art,* Fonds Mercator, Antwerp 1981.

Valentin Vermeersch (ed.), *Bruges and Europe,* Fonds Mercator, Antwerp 1992.

Herman Liebaers, Valentin Vermeersch, Leon Voet, Frans Baudouin, Robert Hoozee et al., *Flemish Art From the Beginning Till Now,* Fonds Mercator, Antwerp 1985.

I also found a great deal of very useful information in the detailed Policy Memorandum 1999–2004 *Memlingmuseum–Sint-Janshospitaal en Museum Onze-Lieve-Vrouw ter Potterie (Stedelijke Musea Brugge),* drawn up by Curator Hilde Lobelle-Caluwé with the assistance of Stefaan Traen and Eva Tahon.

© 2001 Ludion, Ghent-Amsterdam
and Irene Smets
Translation: Ted Alkins
Design: Antoon De Vylder,
Herentals
Typesetting: De Diamant Pers,
Herentals
Colour separations and printing:
Die Keure, Bruges
D/2001/6328/04
ISBN: 90-5544-307-7

Hans Memling,
*Triptych of St John the Baptist
and St John the Evangelist,* detail (see p. 37).